The Ontario Residential Real Estate How-To Book

The Ontario Residential Real Estate How-To Book

Lessons In Residential Real Estate in Ontario That Will Save You Time, Money & Headaches

Another Great Book by Award-Winning Author, Dr. Christine Topjian

Christine Topjian Publishing

CONTENTS

PART vii
PART ix
DEDICATIONS xi

Introduction

Glossary

1 Why Invest In Real Estate In Ontario? 11

2 Residential Real Estate In Ontario 15

3 Solid Financial Choices 21

4 Renting Out Your Property In Ontario 29

5 Look-Fors When Buying A Property 37

6 Working With Great Tenants 44

7 Rental Documents In Ontario & How To Complete Them Fully & Correctly 48

8 Repairs & Working With Tradespeople 51

9 The Landlord & Tenant Board 55

CONTENTS

10 | Tithing 57

11 | A Last Note 59

FOR SERVICES 63
NOTES 65

The Ontario Residential Real Estate How-To Book: Lessons In Residential Real Estate in Ontario That Will Save You Time, Money & Headaches

"Check out the many books by Award-winning Author, Dr. Christine Topjian at DrChristineTopjian.com"

Other books by Dr. Christine Topjian (and counting):

Jesus Loves You

Love & Kindness

Give it to God

Hannah Can Read

It's in Transit

How to Be Led by the Holy Spirit

Are You Ready for God's Best for Your Life?

The Chrissie Series: Chrissie Meditates & Visualizes

The Chrissie Series: Chrissie Goes Places

The Chrissie Series: Chrissie Prays

CONTENTS

The Chrissie Series: Chrissie Speaks Nicely

The Power of the Give

God & Prosperity

Manifest It!

Manifest It ... Now!

Etes-vous prêts pour le meilleur de Dieu?

THE MONEY MANUAL

The Art of Getting It Done

DEDICATIONS

This book is dedicated to Dave.

Introduction

Knowledge is power.

Learning and understanding are power.

They are all critical to success!

In this book, we are going to be talking exclusively about residential real estate in Ontario. We will not be talking about commercial real estate in this book because residential real estate is such a vast and important field on its own that it deserves its own book. Also, the commercial real estate market is very different and has its own set of rules and regulations, very few of which will be touched on in this book.

I spent years not knowing enough but being involved in residential Ontario real estate. An unfortunate thing happens when you don't know enough and you haven't taken enough time to learn the ropes: you end up being taken advantage of. That's a scary thing to happen in any industry - no less so in real estate, where we are dealing with property, capital, monthly payments and significant amounts of money. It is therefore essential to know the rules that govern Ontario residential real estate and yes, as the rules change substantially, this book will be updated from time to time over the years to reflect those changes.

> Read up on the rules because not knowing will cost you.

So....dear reader, learn. Absorb. Read up on the rules because not knowing will cost you. You will want and need to know your rights in order to be able to properly and successfully navigate and operate in this landscape.

And of course, with this knowledge comes increased income, increased self-confidence, more strategic and wise moves and overall, knowing your stuff and feeling really good about that.

When I was getting started in residential real estate, I had read a little bit (actually, a lot) from books that were already on the market. Unfortunately, those books did not (hindsight is 20-20) reflect the reality I would come to experience.

What Made The Difference

God. Jesus. The Holy Spirit. Faith.

I'll say that again: God made the difference. He showed me how the strategies I was using were not helpful and why they were not. **He then showed me and explained to me what the right ways are and how to benefit from those right ways each and every single time.** The proof is in the pudding (so to speak). I have never before experienced the kind of real estate success I experience today (as of the writing of this book in 2022). I accepted and put into practice every single concept, strategy, lesson and warning the Lord showed me and it was quite different from what I had previously been taught.

As add-ons, I am also going to briefly cover the techniques of meditation and visualization as a means of achieving your God-given residential real estate goals (both for living in your home and for using the home as an investment you do not live in). The Bible teaches us that God put in-place and gave us the gifts of being able to pray, meditate and visualize to get everything He has in-store for us. No other book I have ever seen on the market then or now (as of this writing) touches on those critical and essential points and frankly, to not have God and His tools in your corner means that you are already putting yourself at a huge disadvantage.

So, having been an educator for (as of this writing) over 16 years, it is imperative that I cover and explain these items in detail throughout this book. You can learn more about the Holy Spirit and how to be governed by the Holy Spirit in my book, How To Be Led By The Holy Spirit. You can learn more about visualization and manifestation from my books, Manifest It! and Manifest It...Now! You can learn more about the art of getting it done and done well in my book, The Art of Getting It Done: Secrets of Overachievers and How You Too Can Be One.

I also believe that a book that outlines God's ways and goodness is not complete unless it includes Scripture to back it up. This is why I am going to add in Scriptural references as often as I can, and passages that are hopefully going to help "drive home" my point and explain to you how Scripture is as relevant to life today as it was back when it was first written.

> For I know the plans I have for you," declares the LORD, "plans to prosper you and not to harm you, plans to give you hope and a future. (Jeremiah 29:11)

With this Scripture, we can see that God has great plans for each person. It is up to us to be wise enough to tap into this and to see the greatness He is able to do for each of us.

Bearing in mind that not everyone knows all the types of homes available, I have also included a mini glossary at the very beginning to give you those key terms. It may be helpful to highlight them or to print them (or copy them) and stick them up somewhere you will see them again and again.

Happy reading and happy learning!

Glossary

Residence: Where people live. A residence can be any place people live, including but not limited to an apartment, a condo, a townhouse, a semi-detached house, etc. Each type of residence has certain benefits and certain drawbacks, but that is also up to each person's preferences and tastes. For example, many people appreciate that in a condo or an apartment building, you have a garbage system at your disposal that can be used anytime, whereas with a semi or a detached home, you have to cart your garbage to the curb on garbage day (try doing that in -20 degrees Ontario snow conditions).

Apartment: A smaller residence (usually around 500-800 square feet) and located within a building. Some apartment buildings will have such things as a separate room for mailboxes and some may have such services as concierge services.

Condo: This is similar to the apartment structure but condos are usually bigger and are more luxurious. They also usually offer such amenities as a fitness center, a pool and spa, concierge services, a lounge area or areas, party rooms, meeting rooms and a separate location for mailboxes. One of the perceived drawbacks to condo life is that they have condo monthly maintenance fees that need to be paid in order to keep those amenities working and going.

Townhouse: A townhouse is a type of home that is attached to other homes, so it is like a larger version of the condo. Most townhouses have monthly maintenance fees as well, which help take care of expenses like gardening, cable, water and insurance. The only type of townhouse that has very low monthly maintenance fees are freehold townhouses. Townhouses are managed and governed by an elected board of directors who volunteer their time and energy for the position for the benefit of all the owners.

Semi-Detached: This is a house that has one side attached to one other half of a house (so it is like 2 parties are sharing one larger house). With a semi-detached, you don't have the monthly maintenance fees, but only half the house belongs to you so you can't do what you want to do with the whole house (ex. If you want to renovate).

Detached: This is a stand-alone house where, as an owner, you are responsible for everything to do with the house, from garden maintenance, to snow removal to to taking out the trash on garbage day. There are no monthly maintenance fees with this so you are going to pay your garbage and solid waste management utilities directly to the city. Unless you are in a private, gated community, you have no concierge or anything like that.

Mortgage: A mortgage is a monthly payment you make to the bank or to a financial institution as a cost of borrowing for the value of the house. For example, if you bought the house for $800,000 CDN and you put down a down payment of $100,000, you will have to pay mortgage interest on $700,000 (the amount you borrowed from the bank or FI). If your monthly mortgage interest rate is 2.5%, your monthly mortgage amount will be

Mortgage payment: This is the dollar amount you have to pay each month as a penalty for borrowing from the bank or the FI.

Interest rate: This is the percentage rate you will have to pay each month as a penalty for borrowing from the bank or the FI. These vary depending on the FI you select, but generally, interest rates are pretty high.

Tenant: This is the person who is renting the home from the owner. They pay monthly to rent the space and must sign a lease so that the Tenant and the Landlord are both in agreement with the terms of the lease.

Landlord: This is the person who owns the home and if they have chosen to rent out the home, they become the renter's landlord. They must sign a lease so that the Tenant and the Landlord are both in agreement with the terms of the lease.

Landlord and Tenant Board: This is the government body that sets out the rules and the laws of all residential leases in Ontario. They make laws and when there is a dispute, they provide free information to both Landlords and Tenants. The rules here heavily favor the Tenants.

RTA (Residential Tenancy Act): This is the standard law of Ontario that says what may be included in a lease and what may not.

Appreciating (in value): A home may appreciate in value, meaning that the value of the home increases as time goes on. For example, a home may today be worth $800,000 CDN but because of appreciation, next year, that same home could be worth $1,000,000 CDN. Obviously for the homeowner, they desire for their home to appreciate in value.

Depreciating (in value): A home may depreciate in value, meaning that the value of the home decreases as time goes on. For example, a home may today be worth $800,000 CDN but because of depreciation, next year, that same home could be worth $$600,000 CDN. Obviously, the homeowner does not want this.

Capital: This is money you plan to use to buy the home.

Principal: This is the dollar amount you (as a purchaser of a home) put down to begin to pay for the home. Some banks and FI ask for a certain minimum percentage to be put down before they will grant you a mortgage.

Big Ticket Items: There are some items in a home that are very high in dollar value and will be very high in ticket value, so when you are looking to buy (or even rent) a home, it is important to pay attention to all of the following: the furnace, the roof, and the foundation.

MLS: This stands for multiple listing service, which is the online service that lists all the properties in Ontario for rent or for sale. Each listing includes such basic information as the home's address (and unit number, if applicable), pictures, how much it is being sold or the asking rent, features of the home such as basement, water source, cable source and remarks to explain the details of the home. If the listing is being put up by a brokerage, the name and contact information of the real estate agent will be included here.

Realtor.ca: This is another online listing service that is almost the same as MLS. Generally, when one listing is on MLS, it will also be on realtor.ca. This website usually has the same amount of information as would be on an MLS listing.

Real estate agent: This is an agent who represents one's interests for a property. A real estate agent can represent any party to any real estate transaction. For example, an owner who wants to lease or sell their property can have a real estate agent and a buyer or tenant can also have a real estate agent to buy or lease the property. It is always the owner/landlord who pays for the agent's services, for himself or herself and for the buyer or tenant. The governing body for real estate agents is OREA (Ontario Real Estate Association) - they are the ones that regulate agents, hold them to standards of professionalism, etc.

Offer to lease: This is an offer a prospective tenant brings to the owner, indicating that they want to lease their property and the terms of that lease. The prospective tenant can have a real estate agent working with them to represent (negotiate) their interests or they can not.

Offer to purchase: This is an offer a prospective buyer brings to the owner, indicating that they want to buy their property and the terms of that sale. The prospective buyer can have a real estate agent working with them to represent (negotiate) their interests or they can not. In this type of transaction, it is advisable that both sides have a real estate agent working for them because there are legal aspects to this that are very intricate and important.

Rental income: This is the monthly income the landlord will receive from the tenant in exchange for the tenant living in their property.

Utility bill(s) for solid waste and garbage removal: These are specific to Ontario properties and they are charged once every three or so months. These bills come directly from the city for solid waste and garbage removal services.

Other utility bills: These are the other utility bills that come from such companies as Hydro.

1

Why Invest In Real Estate In Ontario?

The first item I would like to cover in this book is why even bother investing in real estate? There are many other investment vehicles and options available. Why real estate?

Here are some reasons:

- Real estate in Canada always increases in value (save for some small dips in the market)
- Real estate can help you grow your money (the value of your home today is $600,000, in a year it could be $800,000)
- Everyone needs to live somewhere. Would you rather live in your own home or in someone else's?
- Building equity - each time you purchase a home or each time you make mortgage payments, you are increasing the equity available in your home. The more equity you have, the better.
- You would be increasing your financial knowledge and know-how.
- While you are going to work and earning money, the money you already earned and invested in the home is also working for you.

- Biblically, it is wise financial stewardship to own your own property and to invest your money.
- Real estate gives you another outlet for relying on God and His provision.

Real estate and real estate investing is a very vast and very complicated industry. In order to navigate oneself within it in an intelligent way, we need to be well read and learned about it. This takes time and as such, if you are new to the field, start learning as soon as possible.

Property Values

If you have ever taken the car out for a spin and decided to spend some time going through neighborhoods and checking out what is what, you may be seeing a plethora and array of homes that may look similar, some may look different, some neighborhoods will be better than others and some districts have different offerings (ex. Downtown Toronto tends to offer a more edgy and funky scene while uptown Toronto is more serene and has much less in terms of bars and nightclubs). There are stunning areas and locations all over Toronto and all over Ontario but if you are looking for specific value offerings, you have to know where to look. For example, if being by the water is very important to you (and maybe your family) then searching by areas that have no water will be less meaningful to you.

Property values will vary widely in Ontario and it is important to check out home listings to get a sense of where property values are. You might want to check free newspaper listings and there is a ton of information online regarding how much properties of all types are selling for or are being leased for.

Do the property values of some areas increase at a faster rate than other areas? Of course because some areas have stronger value offers such as clean spaces to live, sanitary parks, amenities and places to buy groceries, apparel, furniture and more, some places are near the water and so they have some of the highest valuations, homes near really well-run and well-managed schools are also very important and increase in value at greater rates. These homes are ones that boast more value for your dollar.

Lot Size

The size of a property's lot is really important and goes quite a way in helping to determine its value. Generally, the bigger a property's lot size, the higher its value therefore the greater price tag it will command. I say that because when it comes to pricing a property, it is more often than not the comparables that are looked at and the property will be priced accordingly. The lot size tells just how much property and land value you are getting ownership of so it is a very important consideration.

The lot size information will generally be found on the factual information page for any property. It will contain the exact lot size so when you get hold of this information, don't lose sight of it. Why? Because one day, it may be called into question and you will need that documentation to back up your claims. Further, it helps determine where your land ends and that of your neighbours' begins.

Ravines

Having a ravine or a small forest next to or behind your home is also a very attractive attribute. People generally love being near such nature

ANOTHER GREAT BOOK BY AWARD-WINNING AUTHOR, DR. CHRISTINE TOPJIAN

and ravines provide an awesome amount of clean air, something that if your own primary home does not offer, you may be tempted to buy a cottage in a space that is open-air.

2

Residential Real Estate In Ontario

Residential real estate in Ontario is such an awesome and fascinating field.

It is fun, interesting, and there are many rules you need to know about before you make arguably the most important purchase of your life: that of your home. Not knowing the rules will really work against you and even if you have already made your first purchase without having acquired the full knowledge needed, it is not too late to go, read up, learn and understand what is going on. Going forward, you will be able to make better quality decisions with your newfound knowledge, possibly better decisions than you have made so far.

Residential real estate encompasses apartments, condos, townhouses (both freehold and regular), semi-detached, detached, mobile homes, and water-based homes (like boats). Each has their value within the residential real estate landscape and each has its own best practices. For example, one of the residential homes listed will be the best option to serve you and your family over another, and that particular type of property will have its own set of rules, laws and ways to acquire it and manage it that make it unique from the others.

Buying your home is a very important decision and investment. I think we can all agree on that. When it comes to important investments like this, it is vital that we are properly informed about all of the following:

- Taxes (and how tax rates go up every 4 years)
- Mortgage rates (and how these have changed over the years)
- Capital available to invest as down payment
- Monthly maintenance fees
- Repair costs
- City planning and the changes that will cause for your neighborhood and area

In sum, know what you are buying and what you are signing up for! Not knowing is not going to help you later on. Buying a property is, for some, an emotional decision, but unlike with emotional decisions, this one requires a sound, cool mind, proper information and calculations, Holy Spirit-led reasoning and realistic expectations. For example, you can go ahead and purchase a home that is at or over-budget but please don't forget about the other expenses you will have coming at you which also need to be factored into the price of the home:

* taxes
* home maintenance expenses
* monthly mortgage expenses

Each month, these expenses will come out of your account and yes, your bank balance will be decreasing by the amount you owe. Further, all of these expenses will continue to rise (they only go up, they don't really ever come down), because cost of living in Ontario always increases, never decreases. So, if your interest rate today is 2.5%, tomorrow it will likely be higher in a year from now, meaning that you will owe more as you sign on for higher rates because that is what the market is calling for. Similarly, monthly maintenance fees always go up and things always become more expensive to repair and/or replace. Property managers (those who manage residential properties for owners in a townhouse) don't work for free. All of these costs need to be factored in when you are considering a purchase.

Basically, we need to go in with all the knowledge possible and with a cool head.

The Story of Ada

I'd like to share the story of Ada, a woman I know, to illustrate the previous point about avoiding emotional purchases. Ada was about to get married and she and her husband were looking for their ideal home. They both had good jobs but they were both fairly new to not only the residential marketplace but also to their jobs. Ada and her husband decided they wanted to "live large" and buy a big, beautiful house to go along with their two luxury cars (one for each of them). Because they were both new to the marketplace, they both only looked at the acquisition price of the house. Their real estate agent did not clarify for them that this was just the beginning of the expenses - and that other expenses would soon follow. Ada and her husband had also taken out a large mortgage because they had heard from friends that you shouldn't put too much down, but instead, "let the bank put the money in". They were thrilled to hear this line of thinking because they thought it meant more money in their pockets. So, they went ahead and purchased a large townhouse property in an upscale area of Toronto.

By the time they got the deed in their hands, the lawyer who closed the deal for them also notified that the interim taxes (meaning the taxes for the first half of the year) would be coming up due, as would the monthly maintenance fees. Their home acquisition cost $1.2 million, their monthly maintenance fees were over $800 per month because a shared swimming pool, fitness area and concierge were included and then, they needed to know that the actual tax amount was just an estimate, and that that amount was subject to increase based on the house's actual square footage. They were in over their heads.

My reason for telling you the story of Ada and her husband is so that you see that the acquisition cost of the property is just the beginning. There are many other expenses that will be coming up and that are non-negotiables - they have to be paid unless you want to lose the home (in Canada, this is called the property going into power of sale while in the US, it is called a property foreclosure). Ada and her husband were in over their heads and I don't want to tell you how Ada also decided that luxury vacations would be required for them too, adding further strain on their finances and their marriage.

Types of Homes & Descriptions

There are fine but important differences in the structures and therefore the rules, setups and administration of each. We will go into each of them in detail because those details are going to dictate maintenance fees implications, structural and renovation implications, and much more.

Here are some of the different types of homes available in Ontario and how to learn the differences between apartments, townhouses, condos, semis or fully detached homes:

Apartment: A part of a house or a building or structure that is occupied by one person or people, while another part of the house or building or structure that is occupied by another person or set of people. Apartments are generally on the more economical side of things. Apartments almost always have monthly maintenance fees attached.

Condo: Same type of unit structure as an apartment but the people who live here are owners of the space. Condos are generally a bit nicer and more luxurious than apartments.

* One of the biggest differences between a condo and an apartment is the ownership: apartments are usually rented by the occupant while condos are owned by the occupant.

Semi-detached: A semi-detached house is a single family duplex dwelling house that shares one common wall with the next house. The name distinguishes this style of house from detached houses, with no shared walls, and terraced houses, with a shared wall on both sides.

Detached: A stand-alone house is a free-standing residential building. It is sometimes referred to as a single-family home, as opposed to a multi-family residential dwelling.

Condo Townhouse: A condo townhouse means that you own everything inside of the unit's structure, while the exterior is owned and maintained by a condo corporation. This can include common areas on the property, parking spaces, and the yard.

Freehold Condo Townhouse: Simply put, a freehold townhome is a house that is attached on both sides and has the same features as a detached house. What this means is that there are no extra management fees, no common areas, and no condo association fees.

Now that you know a bit more about the different options available to you vis-a-vis the residential market, you can make more informed financial decisions about which one is right for you, whether to live in it or to rent it out. We are going to talk about solid financial choices in the next chapter, including your mortgage and payments. For more information about money matters, you can pick up my book, THE MONEY MANUAL which teaches quite a bit on setting a budget, managing your finances and more.

3

Solid Financial Choices

People of all ages need to learn about and make informed and solid financial choices. This is a basic vital life skill. This is going to be, arguably, one of the most important financial decisions you make, and you cannot make wise financial decisions and choices when you are not well-informed.

I will include here another reminder that was given to me many years ago (way before I ever got involved with real estate): check your emotions at the door. Allow me to explain: I understand that buying a property can be a very exciting and emotional decision but you need to check your emotions at the door. The reason I say that is because many people make emotional home buying decisions without being conscious and mindful of what they are really getting themselves into, and the associated costs and expenses that need to be factored in. Being overly emotional is basically saying "I want this property no matter what - I don't care about how much and I don't care about what the home comes with, I just want it!"

In my earlier example of Ada and her husband, they got a bit emotionally attached and did not make the most sound financial choices, they did not ask all the questions they needed to up-front and they did not factor in all the expenses they would be incurring. They ended up paying for it with their bank accounts, their emotions and their marriage. Today, unfortunately, they are no further ahead with their finances and their costs have mounted. Today, they continue to pay for their home by taking on more and more loans and by using their credit cards (I definitely advise against that).

Losing your home to foreclosure in Canada is not uncommon and can happen when people don't go into this investment decision with both eyes wide open!

So, how do we make solid financial choices?

Simple: Get informed. Write out all your expenses and income. Be very realistic. Ask God to open your eyes to what you need to be seeing and paying attention to.

Get informed by understanding the market, reading up on market trends, talking to different people, seeing the prices in newspapers and online and learn the ropes and the terminology.

Writing out all the costs that you will be facing is incredibly important. Here is the basic schema for your expenses. You are more than welcome to use this schema and to slot in your particular information or to make amendments to it so that it more closely reflects your particular context:

Be very realistic about everything from your expenses (you will have other expenses besides this property) and your income today and tomorrow. Bear in mind that as you move through life, you will have more expenses so the expenses you factor in today will likely grow. Also remember that financial institutions regularly change their interest rates so ask yourself if you will be able to afford a higher interest rate in a few years.

Ask God for His help. When we humble ourselves and go to God for help and for guidance, we are acknowledging that we need His help (which is excellent). When we think we can go it alone, we will run into additional difficulties, and we won't have Him working with us to help us through them.

Now, bear in mind that this formula and these givens are for purchases only. We only put a down payment when we are purchasing a property:

Capital being put down as a down payment:

Mortgage interest rate:

Monthly maintenance fees (if any):

Tax payments for the year:

Land transfer tax:

Capital Down Payment

The capital you put down on your home as a deposit is very important and it **should be as much as you (and your spouse or partner) can afford**. Simply put: you want to put down as much as possible here because when you borrow from the bank, you are paying interest on every cent borrowed. So, if the house is worth $1,000,000 and you put down $30,000,000, you will be paying interest (at whatever percentage your interest rate is) on $70,000.

Let's say your interest rate is 3.00%, the amount you will be paying in interest each month is:

$70,000 x 3.00% = $2,100 interest value you will be paying each month

Let's say that you are in a home that requires the payment of maintenance fees and your maintenance fees are $650 per month. That means that in addition to taxes, and mortgage payments, you will have $650 taken out of your bank account each month for maintenance. Keep in mind that I have not yet factored in taxes or repair expenses.

The amount of your down payment is very important. Your down payment is the amount you are putting down toward the full payment of your home. Basically, the more you put in as a down payment, the more quickly you stand a chance to pay off your home. Many people I spoke to at the beginning of my real estate journey erroneously told me that putting down the least amount for your down payment is smart because you should "let the bank pay for it." Wrong. Put in as much as you can for your down payment so that you can pay off that home sooner rather than later because every penny you borrow from a bank or a financial institution is going to carry interest with it. Interest means more money out of your pocket and more money in the institution's.

First Time Homebuyers Credit

Many financial institutions offer to help first time homeowners become so with the help of financial relief. It is really important to make sure you ask your financial institution about whether you would qualify for this, if you are a first-time homebuyer, regardless of the type of home you are looking to buy. Why? Because any financial discount and incentive is better than none.

I also want to remind you that this is only available for a first-timer, not someone who already owns a home. Does it mean that if you and your spouse or partner are buying a home and that one of you two are a first-time buyer that they can get the credit? Yes. As long as the person has never bought a property before, they get this financial incentive.

Coming Up With the Down Payment

Put very simply, you need as much money as possible for your down payment. This means that as soon as you can begin working and saving money, you should do so. Down payments can take some time to accumulate and if you are not working hard and strategically to get the money together, then you are going to fall short later. People who are mindful with their finances tend to do all of the following or try to do all of the following:

- Make money as soon as possible
- Save your money earned
- Live at home as long as you can so that you are saving (even if you, say, live at home with your folks and pay some rent, that is still likely to be cheaper than going on your own and paying full rent and utilities)
- Invest money in safe and secure assets like bonds (bonds may have low return interest rates but your principal is guaranteed - in other words, you won't lose the money you put in)
- No need to spend regularly on such expensive things like takeout, delivery and such. You can treat yourself every now and then

but when you do this frequently, you are wasting the money you could have been saving
- Work in industries where tips are provided
- If you are a creator of any kind, you can enter contests and competitions, especially ones that pay the winner
- If you will be getting a place, having a roommate who can share the costs with you would be really helpful (provided you get along well with them)
- Create products and services that are their own and for which other people will pay them
- Learn to invest in the stock market in an intelligent way

I think you get the point that it is important to learn how to make and save your money as early as possible. Teaching financial literacy to all ages is so important and everyone at all ages needs to know how and to be mindful of making and saving money. It also is important to know that while it would be nice to have the nicest of everything (clothes, home, car, etc.) that this is not the way to financial prosperity. Everything costs and we need to remember that costs can mount very quickly.

Mortgage Terms

When the financial institution gives you the paperwork for the mortgage terms, please take the time to read through everything and ask tons of questions. The mortgage terms are very important because they will dictate what you can and cannot do during the entire length of your mortgage. If you are not able to meet those demands, don't sign for the mortgage because the financial institution will hold you to those terms once you have signed the papers.

Pre-payment terms is one aspect in particular to pay close attention to in the mortgage document. The pre-payment terms tell you how much you are able to put in at a time. Some mortgages do not allow for any pre-payments because these will end up potentially lowering your monthly costs. Some financial institutions don't want you to pay less so they either provide you with no pre-payment limits or limited ones.

I always use my phone to jot down the dates for prepayments and to know what I owe and what I can pay into my mortgage.

Credit Cards

This chapter on solid financial choices would be incomplete without my talking about credit cards. Use your credit card but **use it wisely,** and by that, I mean make purchases but at the end of the month, pay the whole thing off. Many people make the mistake of living beyond their means and charging things to their card or cards, only paying off the monthly minimum each month. I would highly advise against doing that. If you don't pay off the entire amount, you are going to be accumulating and paying interest on the amount not yet paid off. This means that, let's say, the piece of furniture that you purchased for $1200 and which you put on your credit card (which has an interest rate of, say, 30%) is going to be accumulating monthly interest of 30% x $1200 = $360 per month. That means the following:

In month 1 of not paying off that piece of furniture, you now owe $1,560.

In month 2 of not paying off that piece of furniture, you now owe $1,920.

In month 3 of not paying off that piece of furniture, you now owe $2,280.

In short, instead of saving your money, you are now paying well over the $1200 price for that couch.

The best thing to do is to pay off the amount immediately (when it is due) in full. If you do that, you will not have to pay interest and you will be building good credit and you will get the points for the purchase on your credit card.

Financial Literacy

Financial literacy is for everyone. If you are not yet comfortable with financial literacy, allow me to advise you to get comfortable with it and to learn, learn, learn. Your relationship with money matters. It matters today, tomorrow and will always matter. If you do not take proper care of your finances, not only will you be suffering as a result of poor choices but so may the rest of your family who may have to make up for the shortfalls.

Take some time each day and get more financially literate. It is a learning process that lasts a lifetime. I don't know of anyone (myself included) who is not still learning and still growing in this area!

4

Renting Out Your Property In Ontario

"Becoming a landlord in Ontario is not for the faint of heart"
This was said to me many years ago by an agent in the industry and it is one of the truest statements ever uttered. In real estate, and especially when you are a landlord, you not only have to be incredibly thick skinned and strategic, but you have to know what your rights and your responsibilities are and you have to be able to navigate the system wisely.

Renting your residential property in Ontario can be very treacherous but it also has its advantages. Some of the advantages include:

- Having someone live in and look after your home
- The rental income which can help with your own monthly payments
- Your insurance rates to insure the home will usually be lower when there is someone living in it because when someone lives in it, the chances for an unmonitored disaster are much less
- The pipes in your home will be used regularly (if they are not, the pipes can get backed up and/or burst)

Realistically speaking, one of the greatest advantages to renting out your home is the monthly rent coming in. It is helpful because this amount renews each month and helps you pay your mortgage, your taxes and more.

How We Deal the Holy Spirit In

If you deal the Holy Spirit out of the equation, whether you consider yourself to be a "religious person" or not, you are already at a disadvantage. The Holy Spirit will tell you things about the context, the property, and anything else that you would not ever have known without God telling you about it. So how do we deal the Holy Spirit in? Simple. Pray. Here is a suggested prayer you may want to use to help you invite the Holy Spirit (the Spirit of God) into your real estate situation: *"Dear God, I feel I need Your help in this area of my life. I am learning about real estate and I am asking You to guide me with Your wisdom and Your infinite knowledge. Please guide me in ways so that I will know it is You and make Your guidance clear to me. I thank You ahead of time for Your answer to this prayer. In Jesus' name. Amen"*

After praying that prayer (or a version of it), quiet yourself and listen carefully to any sensations, feelings, inklings or communications you feel you may be getting. That will be the Holy Spirit speaking to you, helping you, guiding you and answering your prayers. Pay attention to this guidance and if you want my take, write down all the guidance you get so you can be clear about it and refer back to it later too.

What some people do sometimes is that they don't listen carefully to what the Holy Spirit is saying, they make independent decisions and then when things don't work out the way they hoped they would, they get mad at God. It can't work that way because that isn't fair. If He is speaking and you are not listening carefully or you have not written the guidance down carefully, then you cannot blame Him. Instead, go back to Him in prayer, ask where you may have gone wrong and see what He says about fixing the situation. He will always answer and help.

Hiring An Agent Or Going It Yourself

So, you have either made the decision to become a landlord or you are strongly considering it and you may be feeling like the Holy Spirit is or has been guiding you to take on this role. Ok. My first question is: will you be doing this on your own or will you hire a real estate agent to represent you?

I will provide the pros and cons of each so that you can make an informed, Holy Spirit-led decision.

Pros of hiring an agent:

- You have a professional who has been in the industry, passed all the legal requirements and knows how to handle the transaction to be working for you
- They will advise you through all of it, helping you each step of the way
- They will handle the paperwork for you and the legal documentation
- They will take you to see the properties and walk you through everything you are seeing

Cons of hiring an agent:

- Sometimes an agent is working for their interests more than yours (ex. Encouraging you to make a purchase or rent a place that is over your budget)
- As a landlord, sometimes your agent may not tell you the red flags that they see in a property or in a potential tenant
- Sometimes agents will not explain things to you or to the other party correctly, which could put into jeopardy the entire transaction
- Agents are expensive to use
- They don't always fill things out correctly or thoroughly (I have experienced this more with agents I have hired many times)

Pros of being your own agent:

- You control every part of the transaction
- You keep your money (to listing agent to pay)
- You can negotiate best for your interests (if you know the rules)
- You can list the property yourself
- If you do the showing for the prospect, you will be able to get a sense of the person firsthand (without relying on your agent to tell you things)

Cons of being your own agent:

- You will have to do the work yourself
- If you don't know the rules, you will not be negotiating as effectively as is needed
- You may make a mistake with your paperwork if you are not sure of what you are doing and this could nullify the whole deal
- You may not wish to meet the prospect face to face

If you have made the decision to do this on your own, you will need to list the property in a clear and well done manner. This means your pictures are clear and up to date, the area and home descriptions are clear and on-point, and you have all the information needed such as how many bedrooms, bathrooms, where the washer & dryer are, parking spaces on the driveway and in the garage, utilities info, nearby schools, and more. There are certain sites where you can list your property in order for it to be seen and considered by potential tenants or buyers. You can go about this in a few ways. Here they are:

Kijiji.ca

Listedbyseller.ca

Zoocasa.com

Zillow.com

Some of the sites listed have a charge to them but to be honest, when there is a small charge, it usually means the quality of the service will be a little bit better.

When You Are An Owner And You Have An Agent

When you are working with an agent and you are looking for the right buyer or tenant, your agent will list the property for you on either MLS or on Realtor.ca and will take care of all the listing details.

Properly Get To Know Potential Tenants

Any of the websites I have mentioned here can be very helpful and effective in finding the right tenant but you will need to screen tenants properly in order to find the right tenant for you. This means following up on all their references, seeing if they are actually employed at the company they claim to work for, seeing what their previous landlords have to say about them, etc. I recall a rental application I received where I called to follow up on what their previous landlord had to say about them. The person kindly answered the call, identified themselves as the landlord of that address, but when I mentioned the names of the people listed on the rental application, the person said that he did not have tenants by those names. The landlord references given were false information.

Another time I received a call from an agent who asked me if I was the owner of the property. When I confirmed that I was, they asked if I had ever had a tenant by the name of so and so. I again confirmed that I did. She was calling because her client (the landlord) had received a rental application from my former tenants who had walked out of thousands they owed me and had falsified the information on the rental application, providing an alternate owner's name on the property.

The right tenants will be kind, respectful, have their papers in order, will be truthful with you about everything from the beginning, and will work with you each step of the way to ensure that there are no misunderstandings and that you are both on the same page. Their agent, if they choose to use one, will be the same.

I recall an agent who called me regarding a listing and while she initially came off very kindly, once the negotiations began and she saw that she was not getting her way with everything, she became exceptionally rude. I have found that when that happens, it is not the right cooperating agent to be working with nor is it likely the right potential tenant.

Home Owners...The Responsibility Is Yours

The tenants who have uncaring attitudes will end up costing you because the ultimate responsibility of everything to do with the home ultimately rests on your shoulders. Neither the city nor the banks or FI care that your tenant is not making their payments, they are not concerned that you don't have the monthly rental income to make your mortgage payments or that your tenant is not making their utility payments. They care about being paid the full amount of what they are owed each month. So be selective and be very choosy about the tenants you take on.

I had a listing I was looking to rent and one man came by with his wife for a showing. They seemed to really like the space and asked if I would not mind waiting there for him to go to the bank and take out the money needed. I advised him that we would need to draw up a proper lease and discuss the terms so I wouldn't be accepting any money. He said he would send in the required documents for the landlord to consider him. We spent a few days discussing the lease and negotiating the terms. On the day the deal was supposed to close and we were supposed to exchange the certified deposit cheque and the keys, he notified me that the cheque he was providing was not certified because it wasn't a personal cheque. When I had mentioned that any cheque can be certified and that a certified cheque would be required, he advised that he was no longer interested in the property. That was good news.

Reader, if you would like to make money in real estate investing - whether that means buying and living in your first home or renting it out or being involved as a real estate agent or just being renting out spaces you already own, I do advise to pay close attention to all of the details mentioned in this book and in other books you read to learn more lessons, see potential pitfalls and much more. Also, certainly, rely on the wise counsel of God, otherwise you are short-changing yourself.

Using An Agent At the Start

If you are new to residential real estate, my suggestion would be to use an agent until you learn the ropes well enough to do it yourself. If you are not new to residential real estate, having an agent can feel like you have someone doing for you what you could be doing for yourself (and saving the money).

5

Look-Fors When Buying A Property

Buying a property is one of the most important financial and life decisions you will make. Properties are expensive and you will be signing up for quite a journey when buying any property.

As such, consult with the Holy Spirit!

Here are some of the ways the Holy Spirit can guide you on your investment journey when you pray for His help and ask:

- Which property is the right one to buy?
- Is this the right time to buy this property or any other?
- Is it God's will for you to be buying now?
- Is it God's will for you to be buying later?
- Should I be working with an agent to represent me in this transaction or should I do this alone since I have a ton of experience?
- What are some costly look-fors that you need to be aware of?
- How much should you offer?
- What terms should you agree to?
- What terms should you negotiate?

- How to ensure that you are getting involved with a legitimate deal, and not one where you are being misled?
- Is the deal you are considering signing the best one for you? For your family?
- Which area is the right one in which to buy or would it be wise to rent first?
- Should you take the home as-is or should you ask for some repairs to be made and included those are part of the deal?

One time in particular where I consulted the Holy Spirit was regarding a deal I was considering entering. Some people around me advised me to take the deal and to not look back but I knew that humans in general are limited in their view and it is the Holy Spirit who can provide a 360 degree explanation and point of view, including most strategic next steps and best decisions. I don't know of any other real estate book that will show you that perspective, which is available to everyone, free of charge!

In my particular situation, I made a decision that was different from what people around me were telling me and I instead went with the guidance of the Holy Spirit, which was different. Hindsight is 20-20 and I can unequivocally say that I made the right decision following the Holy Spirit's guidance.

Mortgages

Taking on a mortgage is not a decision to enter into lightly. It requires careful planning, timeline calculations, and a very honest look at one's realistic financial position. A mortgage with a high interest rate can be very hazardous to your health and your pocketbook.

In a mortgage agreement, you are promising and guaranteeing that you will make consistent, monthly payments to the bank or the financial institution for years to come. You are certifying that you will be making these payments consistently and without defaulting. These payments are over-and-above your taxes, your maintenance fees (if you live in an apartment, condo or townhouse) and any repair expenses you will need to make. Bear in mind that you have to pay your mortgage each month - banks (especially during the time of covid) may offer you "mortgage vacations" and some such but in the end, be in the know that you will be paying for those little "vacations". Understand well if these little vacations will entail your being asked to pay penalties, your being asked for additional fees and, or how the little vacation will affect you in the long run. Yes, being late with your mortgage payment is a breach of contract and it will cost you.

When you are shopping around for your mortgage, bear in mind what the terms of the mortgage you are signing up for are, and bear in mind the interest rate. This is the percentage amount you will be paying each and every single month, so you are looking to get as low a mortgage interest rate as possible.

Someone once asked me if it's ok to negotiate a lower interest rate with a bank. The answer is most definitely yes! In fact, it is your right and your responsibility to do so. A mortgage is a two-way agreement, one where you are agreeing to terms with the financial institution. In any contractual agreement, you must know that you can negotiate the terms.

Buying a property is usually a sound investment. Historically, real estate values have done very well for their owners over many years, with market values increasing on a regular basis (at least in Canada). Even when there have been dips, the market recovers and we continue on with this solid investment. There are, however, some key look-fors. In other words, there are some important items we need take into consideration as being big-ticket items that one would need to take into consideration and look at carefully before even placing an offer on a home. I have used home inspectors before and their services can be quite helpful, but you (as the buyer) need to be aware as well. You need to know what you're getting yourself into and how to navigate this landscape.

Here are some important (and expensive) look-fors:

- Age and condition of the roof
- Age and condition of the furnace
- Are there issues with the home's foundation?
- Has the home been waterproofed?
- Are there any signs of mold?
- Check on the zoning (Is it residentially zoned? Commercially zoned?)
- Is it near a police department, fire station or school?

I will never forget forgoing an inspection of a house I was looking at. I will never make that mistake again because there was significant mold, significant foundation issues and more. No matter how "hot" the market is and how much you may be tempted to put in an offer because you love the home, a thorough home inspection is very important and cannot be overlooked. I understand that, especially when the market is hot, we can get excited and we can get into the mentality of "I WANT that home!!" especially when there is a bidding war. We do, however, have to take a step back and consider that while the home may be great, we have to go in with eyes wide open. Just because the home is in a bidding war situation, it does not stop the home from being subject to the same pitfalls as any other.

Lining Up Your Mortgage

It isn't a great idea to leave your mortgage application just before you put in your offer or worse, just after you put in an offer to purchase. If you don't put any conditions on your offer, you are telling the agent and the seller that you have all your financial ducks in order and that you are able to purchase the home without issue.

Mortgages, as I mentioned further up, both their terms and their rates, are subject to negotiation. You have to do your homework and you have to make sure that you are getting the most competitive rates available. This does require forward planning and leg work. The time to do that is even before you begin looking at potential properties for yourself, not right before or right after you have put in your offer.

You will also need to see if your mortgage is a closed (or fixed) one or a variable one. I will explain both:

Closed: A closed mortgage is one that cannot be renegotiated, or refinanced before the end of the term without paying a prepayment charge. The monthly payments are fixed for the length of the term and cannot increase or decrease during the entire length of that mortgage contract.

Variable: A variable-rate mortgage, adjustable-rate mortgage, or tracker mortgage is a mortgage loan with the interest rate on the note periodically adjusted based on an index which reflects the cost to the lender of borrowing on the credit markets. The loan may be offered at the lender's standard variable rate/base rate.

Many people on a fixed income believe that a fixed-rate (closed) mortgage is best and it could be, but you also need to remember that with a variable mortgage, if interest rates decrease, the rate will decrease and so you will end up having a much lower payment. For example, if your variable interest rate is 4.2% on a $200,000 mortgage, your monthly payment will be $8,400 but then the rate dips down to 3.2%, your payment for that month dips down to $6,400.

These are things to be aware of and be mindful of when you are doing your shopping homework.

Mortgage Insurance

Many people believe mortgage insurance is very important. I will start by defining what it is. Mortgage insurance is an insurance policy which compensates lenders or investors in mortgage-backed securities for losses due to the default of a mortgage loan. Mortgage insurance can be either public or private depending upon the insurer.

Mortgage insurance is mostly necessary if you intend to or think you will default on your mortgage. Of course, there are circumstances and situations in which this may happen but it is essentially a money-making opportunity for banks and financial institutions.

It would be wise to consider how you can ensure that your mortgage payments will be made on time and in full each month so that you never have to dip into or buy into mortgage insurance. It is very important that you take on a mortgage for your home that you are confident that you will be able to pay and that you have fully planned for.

6

Working With Great Tenants

Great tenants are out there and they are, as the title suggests, great.

Great tenants do all of the following (this is not a completely exhaustive list but it covers many of the most important items):

- Are kind and courteous toward both you and your home
- Take care of your home the way you would
- Notify you of anything needed to be attended to before it becomes a big problem
- Pay the rent on time and in full each month
- Pay their utilities as per your agreed contract
- Speak to you respectfully
- Follow the rules and conduct expectations of the neighborhood, condo corp, etc.
- If they are going to leave, they give proper notice and leave the place in great condition
- Use the space as intended and don't have visitors who stay over for days
- Don't use the space for any other reason than the stated purpose of being a residence

Examples of Great Tenants

Some examples of great tenants I have experienced.

- A lady who was living in my home paid her rent on time and in full each month. She treated me and my place with great respect and only asked me to take care of major repairs if something came up. She didn't call me and complain each time a toilet broke down. She was always kind and courteous and left my home in great shape.
- Another tenant paid on time and was always kind in her relations and communications with me. One time I took too long to get back to her about a repair and so she notified me that she had in fact taken care of the repair and was not charging me for the tradesperson's fee. She took care of it and advised that she was happy to do that.
- A lady and her family had moved in and were very kind about a cheque that had bounced. She not only made sure that the payment was made immediately but also asked if there was something she could do to make it up for me for the inconvenience of that bounced cheque.

Examples of Not-So-Great Tenants

- A tenant that I had not only ran out on the rent but also left a bunch of garbage by the curb, prompting the city to call me and

give me 24 hours to get everything out of there before they served me with a ticket
- A tenant left without paying the rent for several months and promised to pay $500 per month to catch up with the rent. They never paid a single penny.
- A tenant stayed for months rent-free (it's called using the system that heavily favors the tenant) and the landlord couldn't do anything about it.
- A tenant said that they were going to make a payment plan to pay and then never followed through with it. They continue to dodge credit collections agencies.

Setting Up The Contract

How the contractual terms are set up is very important. Everything needs to be set up in clear terms and those terms need to be pointed out and explained to the tenant. Most tenants do not read the contractual terms and just assume they understand everything. It therefore means that the agent has a responsibility to fully explain everything to the person and to make sure that they are in the know and in agreement with everything.

Do not take for granted that either party understands and is in agreement with everything. I can't tell you how many times I have proceeded with a lease only to discover that the terms were not properly explained to the tenant by the cooperating agent and that they were not actually in agreement with all the terms. I find it sad and unfortunate that some agents don't do their job properly and just shove things through. In a real estate rental situation, the two parties (landlord and tenant) have to live with the decisions and the consequences of what they agreed to and have to be in an ongoing, continuous relationship with one another. As such, no matter which side of the equation you are on, I advise you to do your part in ensuring that the agent or agents setting up the deal do so in a manner that is fair and that everyone is explicitly agreeing to.

Great tenants truly are worth their weight in gold. They are also not always the ones who have the best credit scores because things happen to people and some understanding and accommodations are needed. But what is very important are the items I mentioned further up. A great tenant is worth their weight.

7

Rental Documents In Ontario & How To Complete Them Fully & Correctly

There are three rental documents currently (in 2022) needed in Ontario to apply to rent a residential space:

- Rental application
- Letters of employment
- Equifax or TransUnion official credit score

Each of these needs to be filled out completely and totally. They also need to be filled out with factual information that correctly represents the person or people involved. I will explain the purpose of each fully.

Rental Application

The rental application is an important document that provides much-needed information to the potential landlord. It includes such information as the person's last places of residence, how many people and the full names of those who will be living at the property, their professional references, current financial commitments, SIN (that is optional to provide), and why they are looking to move from their current residence.

Some people leave out some pieces of information from the rental application and that isn't something I advise anyone to do. Why? Very simple. The potential new landlord (and their agent if they have one) will not take you seriously and will not choose to rent to you. Fill out everything completely and truthfully and if there are issues that you foresee, let them know about it ahead of time.

Letters Of Employment

This is another important tool to show your potential new landlord that you are a great employee, that you are hard working and that you have been with your employer for some time. Again, having this ready to go to include with your rental application package is really important.

Equifax Or TransUnion Official Credit Score

Please note that I did say official credit score. There are unofficial ones that are out there and can be sent but I do not advise presenting those as they do not present as well as official credit scores. When you are serious about securing a great home to rent, you want to show your best. Even if you know you do not have the best credit, explain that to the potential landlord ahead of time. Not doing so will make it look like you are trying to hide something or cover something up and will not reflect well on you. Being up-front and honest about life situations and circumstances is a lot better than hiding something and then being questioned later.

I remember having had an application in front of me from a party of people who seemed genuine and forthright. When I got further into their paperwork, I discovered that they were not being honest and when I asked them about it, they apologized for having lied and told me the truth. Now, it is up to an individual owner to decide if that is a tenant that you would still consider but I believe in communicating with potential tenants that it is better to be honest than to appear perfect and then we find out otherwise later.

8

Repairs & Working With Tradespeople

This is an important topic and one that needs to be properly and realistically addressed in any real estate book.

Repairs are going to happen and they are inevitable. But working with the right people who will make those repairs in an honest, creative and cost-effective way is essential but the most important point to make in this section is to ask the Holy Spirit who is the right contractor to work with. You, as a human may get a sense of a contractor (and that's great) but asking the Holy Spirit for input and confirmation is essential. I tell you this because I started by not asking and checking in and I paid a hefty price for that error.

I remember working with one contractor who presented himself very well and I was strongly considering working with him. It was not until I checked-in with the Holy Spirit that I discovered that in fact, he had no scruples and that his workmanship was very shabby. Unfortunately, I checked-in with the Holy Spirit after hiring him and his team for a job so that did not go very well when things started to break down and not work as they were supposed to.

Again, there are many repair and renovation companies out there who would love to be hired by you. That does not qualify them. I strongly encourage checking in with the Holy Spirit to find out if they are the right person and the right company to use. This is a decision that will have a far-reaching impact and thousands of dollars, if not more.

In contrast, for another work piece I had, I did check in with the Holy Spirit about another repair and contracting company, to which the Lord provided a big green light. I did give him the work and not only did this person go above and beyond but their prices were also extremely fair. I have never had an issue with any of the work that this person has done.

There is a big difference between good workers and bad ones. Let the Holy Spirit tell you which is which.

Estimates & Materials

It is always wise and important to get a free estimate from the company you are considering using. Estimates give an understanding of the costs you will be facing and not only that, estimates ensure that you know that you are getting good quality products. Some renovators who plan to rent out their property instead of living in them may choose to go a little cheaper on the materials because they won't be living in the property. I understand that. But also remember that at the end of the day, it is your property and cheaper quality materials will not last as long, and may end up costing you more in the long run. Either way, you want the materials and goods to last as long as possible because you paid for them and you want your dollar to have gone further.

I also suggest getting the estimate in writing to your email and in as much detail as possible. I once had a company text me (I find that to be very unprofessional) the estimate and it was so general, it didn't give me a good picture of what to expect.

Buyers and renters both love and appreciate renovations, so remember that whatever you put into the renovation, you should get back and then some. For example, if you do $20,000 of renovations, the value of the property increases by much more than just the $20,000 you put in. It is an investment on your dollar and you should be charging more for having done them.

When I put a listing together and I have done a renovation, I highlight that in the listing and I make it super clear that the space (and which parts) have been renovated. It's a great way to attract people to your home.

Payments For Renovations, Work...Anything

A last but nonetheless important point I'd like to make here about renovations or any work you are going to have done is that you should not be paying for all the work up-front. You can provide a 20%-25% deposit for the contractor's purchase of materials, but you should not be paying 50% or the whole value up-front, in any circumstance.

If you can go personally to see the work being done, then great, do go (both as the work is being done and immediately after). If you cannot, ask the contractor to take videos and pictures and send them to you. You have to see the work done and provide your notes and feedback before paying. That is a non-negotiable.

ANOTHER GREAT BOOK BY AWARD-WINNING AUTHOR, DR. CHRISTINE TOPJIAN

You have to see the work done and provide your notes and feedback before paying.

9

The Landlord & Tenant Board

The Ontario Landlord and Tenant Board is the body that governs and sets out the rules and regulations for residential real estate in Ontario. Its rules affect both landlords and tenants and settle disputes between the two. The rules of the Landlord and Tenant Board stem from the RTA (the Residential Tenancies Agreement) and they provide forms that either party can use to indicate what they would like to do regarding a property. For example, if a tenant would like to indicate to the landlord that there are repairs needed for a home, there is a specific LTB form they can use to notify them formally. If a landlord would like to inform the tenant that they are late with the rent, there is a form for that.

The Forms

I would like to note here that the forms need to be filled out completely and entirely for them to be valid and they also have to be served to the other party properly. If they are not properly served, they risk being invalid and disregarded.

When there is an issue that requires a hearing, due to covid, hearings are now being conducted via zoom. The hearing date will be provided in advance by mail or by email and both parties (both landlord and tenant) will be required to be there. When the hearing happens, unfortunately, it is not a private hearing. There will be others there who will be able to hear the information of the case and yes, this can get very uncomfortable. I recall being in an online hearing and listening to the various cases and situations that were being read out, including people's names and the addresses in question.

When a hearing is complete, the parties will be notified of the Board's decision by email, within a few weeks. These decisions are final but can be appealed within a certain time frame (and there is a cost for filing an appeal and for the original online trial).

I would like to say that the rules at the LTB are fairly written and give equal rights to both sides (landlords and tenants) but that is simply not the case. If either party would like to have legal representation during the online trial, they are of course welcome to do so.

Some Of The Most Important Responsibilities

When you take a look at the LTB website, it is clear that some of the most important responsibilities for the Landlord are to have the place in good working order and to provide the tenant with the tools they will need to maintain the space. The tenant is responsible to make sure that they are paying their rent in full and on time, that they are maintaining the grounds as necessary, and that they are enjoying the space quietly according to city noise rules.

10

Tithing

Tithing, for those who don't know, is a Christian custom of dedicating the first 10% of your income to God and to His good purposes. I sometimes get asked: is this still a custom to be followed? Absolutely yes.

One of the reasons I include this topic in a book about real estate is both because you should be tithing on any real estate income you receive in addition to the fact that many people are looking for more money to make their real estate dreams of home ownership come true.

Look to God.

One of the benefits of tithing is that you are promised that you will receive a return on your money. Scripturally, here is where it speaks about that: (Malachi 3:10)

Bring the whole tithe into the storehouse, that there may be food in my house. Test me in this," says the LORD Almighty, "and see if I will not throw open the floodgates of heaven and pour out so much blessing that you will not have room enough for it.

The passage indicates that you will receive a blessing as a result of your tithing obedience.

From my own personal experience of tithing, I can tell you that this does work and that the Lord does bless in return. Try it and you will see. You can also see wonderful tithing testimonials online at such places like the 700 Club (simply google the 700 Club). When we read testimonials of others, it propels us to do wonderful things for the Lord because we see how He has blessed others.

It Does Take Some Time

Something about tithing that is important to bear in mind is that receiving a return from tithing will not happen overnight. We have to give in faith and in obedience and then we will have to wait a bit for our blessing to come. I would also like to add that we need to wait patiently and with respect, not by consistently asking God "where is my money??" We give because we are giving out of love and respect for God. We give because we also believe He is capable of doing anything. We give because we want to see His purposes accomplished and because He is always doing good for others (ex. Christian soup kitchens). Bear in mind that the organization you are giving to has to have Jesus at its center. If it does not, it does not count as tithes.

11

A Last Note

A Last Note

In real estate as in with life, I advise you to lean on Jesus, the Holy Spirit and the word of God. If you are not very familiar, spend some time reading a simple version of the Bible. Personally, I needed to read a student version of the Bible to help me understand Scripture and to help me understand how to relate that Scripture to my current, everyday life. So, I am a big fan of student Bibles.

God is a God of order. He is a God who helps His children, but you have to know to go to Him and explicitly (either by mouth or in your mind) pray for Him to come into your life and help you. You have to know to get His help and His advice and to hear and feel His guidance through prayer, meditation and stillness. You are unlikely to hear God clearly if you are in loud spaces, and when you are really distracted. (I know I am unable to hear from Him in those ways).

I take time to sit in stillness every day (sometimes a few times a day) to stop. To think. To ask the Lord for His guidance. To reflect on an interaction that just happened and how to strategically deal with it. I take time to ask Him if this is the right way to go and if what I am considering doing is the right way according to Him.

Faith & Real Estate

Again, I am aware that many people would not really associate real estate and faith. Many people would not really understand why or how tithing can help with your real estate dreams but I am here to tell you that God always intended us to rely on Him for everything, real estate included. Many people have made the mistake (me included, originally) to think that they need to go it alone, they have to rely on themselves to get things done. Not so. We are supposed to be working in partnership with Him and we are supposed to be relying on God to do things for us that we simply cannot do as humans.

I am reminded of how one of my favorite pastors, Joel Osteen, talked about how God arranged it for his church to be housed in the huge stadium in which they currently find themselves. He makes it clear that he could not have made that happen in his own strength and abilities - he relied on God to make the deal happen for him to be able to house his church in that huge stadium. It took faith and tithing on Osteen's part.

First Real Estate Book

I would like to note that this is the first book I have written about Ontario residential real estate. I am writing more because I have much more to say through my years of experience and the many, many transactions I have been party to.

It is a fascinating and fun field but it only becomes so when we are well educated and well read on how to navigate the field. If you do not make it your business to know, people today and tomorrow will take advantage of you. You do not need to know everything before you get involved in the field, but you do need to have begun reading, watching, learning and understanding in order to properly navigate the field.

FOR SERVICES

For residential real estate services, check out ChristieRealty.ca

NOTES

This is a section for you where you can write out your thoughts, notes, impressions, prayers and more. Enjoy this section and use it all up as you are reading the book and come back to it often so that you can see your progress over time.

NOTES

NOTES

NOTES

NOTES

NOTES

NOTES

NOTES

NOTES

NOTES

NOTES

www.ingramcontent.com/pod-product-compliance
Lightning Source LLC
Chambersburg PA
CBHW070321120526
44590CB00017B/2765